Alexander V. W Bikkers

Anno Domini 2071

Alexander V. W Bikkers

Anno Domini 2071

ISBN/EAN: 9783742878229

Manufactured in Europe, USA, Canada, Australia, Japa

Cover: Foto ©Andreas Hilbeck / pixelio.de

Manufactured and distributed by brebook publishing software
(www.brebook.com)

Alexander V. W Bikkers

Anno Domini 2071

ANNO DOMINI

2071.

Translated from the Dutch Original,

WITH PREFACE AND ADDITIONAL EXPLANATORY NOTES,

BY

DR. ALEX. V. W. BIKKERS.

LONDON:

WILLIAM TEGG, PANCRAS LANE, CHEAPSIDE.

—

1871.

Watson and Hazell, Printers London and Aylesbury.

TRANSLATOR'S PREFACE.

THE late Artemus Ward was in the habit of quoting—either from his own or another man's store of wit—"Never prophesy unless you know for certain." There is, however, a particular mode of foretelling which is neither dangerous nor venturesome; that process, namely, by which inferences are being drawn from analogous things that have come to pass, and applied to the contemplation of future events. The little book here presented in an English translation may serve as an illustration in point. It was originally published in the Dutch language, the author hiding himself

behind the *nom de plume* of Dr. Dioscorides.
If success goes for anything—and who is
prepared to say what it does *not* go for—we
launch it in its new form with more than
sufficient confidence.   Even within the narrow
geographical limits of the Netherlands it has
rapidly passed through three editions, and a
German scholar has deemed it not unworthy
of a translation in his native tongue.

The present publication is more and at the
same time less than a translation; *more*,
because it has been prepared for a different
class of readers than it was originally intended
for ; *less*, because in some instances, and at one
point especially, we thought we had some
reason to apply the pruning-knife to obnoxious
excrescences, as no doubt they would have
proved in a new soil.   The foot-notes have
either been added with a view to ensure
a perfect understanding on the part of the

reader, or to secure for the little work as wide a circulation as possible. So far with regard to its form, object, and origin. There are the boundaries of *our* province.

A. V. W. B.

London, 1871.

TABLE OF CONTENTS.

ANNO DOMINI 2071.

WHEN comparing the present condition of society with that of past centuries the question naturally arises, what will the future be?

Will the same progress which, in our own times especially, has been of such vast dimensions, and manifested itself in so many directions, *continue to be progressive?* And if so— for who could think of reaction, since the art of printing has guarded against any furrow of the human mind being ever effaced—where is to be the ultimate goal of the progress of our successors? Where are we to look for the fruits of those innumerable germs which the present generation is sowing for the benefit of those that will come after them?

1

These, and similar other questions, occupied
my mind when, seated one afternoon in my
comfortable arm-chair, I allowed my thoughts
freely to wander amid the manes of those that
preceded us. I thought of our own Musschen-
broek, Gravesande, Huyghens, and Stevin, and
of what would be their surprise were they to
reappear on this earth, and gaze upon the
marvellous works of modern machinery; I
passed in review a Newton and Galileo, with
so many others, founders of an edifice which
they themselves would not now recognise. I
thought of steam engines and electric tele-
graphs, of railways and steamboats, of mountain tunnels and suspension bridges, of photography and gasworks, of the amazing strides
lately made by chemistry, of telescopes and
microscopes, of diving bells and aëronautics;
aye, and of a hundred other things, which, in
motley array, wildly crossed my mind, though
all corresponding in this that they loudly
proclaimed the vast and enormous difference
between the present and the past. The line

of demarcation between the one and the other revealed itself still more clearly to me as my thoughts carried me further back into the past and the ghost of Roger Bacon seemed to rise before my imagination. This thirteenth-century child was a scholar who surpassed all his contemporaries in sound judgment and knowledge of natural science; alas! his fate was the ordinary one in store for all those whose light shone above that of others in those darkest of ages. He was accused of witchcraft, and cast into a dungeon, there doomed to sigh for ten weary years, after which, as the rumour goes, he died in his prison. The memory of that illustrious man called to my mind some passages of his writings, from which it will be seen how he, as if endowed with the seer's gift, did actually foretell, some six hundred years ago, that which since, and chiefly in our own time, has become an array of realities. For example:

"It is possible," says he, "to construct spying-glasses by which the most distant objects can be drawn near to us, so that we shall be able to read the most minute writing at an almost incredible distance, to see all kinds of diminutive objects, and to make the stars appear wherever we choose."

*　　*　　*　　*　　*

"We might make waggons that could move along with great velocity, and without being drawn by animals."

*　　*　　*　　*　　*

"Similar other machines might be had, as, for example, bridges without pillars or supports of any kind."

*　　*　　*　　*　　*

"There might be contrivances for the purpose of *navigation without navigators*, so that the greatest vessels would be handled by one single man, and at the same time move onward with greater speed than those with numerous crews."*

* For the original of these passages we refer the scholar to that admirable letter of Bacon's, *De mirabile potestate artis et naturae*, etc., which ap-

As I pondered over such remarkable observations as those, I sank into absolute reverie;
all surrounding objects seemed gradually to
disappear from my sight, until I got into that
peculiar condition in which, while everything
material about us is at rest and passive, the
mind, on the contrary, proves uncommonly
active and alert.

I felt myself suddenly in the midst of an
immense city; *where* I did not know, but
about me I saw a vast square, and in it a
stately edifice with a lofty tower, on which I
fancied I read the following inscription:

A.D. 2071.

JANUARY 1ST.

I could scarcely believe my own eyes, and

peared first of all in the work of Claudius Celestinus,
*De his quae mundo mirabiliter eveniunt, Lutetiae
Parisiorum*, 1542. Bacon's description of a flying
machine, of which we read in the same document,
shows, however, that he too, in his philosophical
visions, was apt to transgress the line of the possi-
bilities.

must have approached the tower with looks highly expressive of curiosity and amazement; for an elderly gentleman, accompanied by a young lady, stepped forward to speak to me. "I see, sir, that you are a stranger in Londinia; if any information could be of service to you——"

These kind words caused me to stop; I looked at the man who stood before me, and was at once struck and impressed by his thoughtful and noble features. Nor was I slow in recognising him. He was the very man with whom I had been for some time past engaged in my thoughts.

"You are Roger Bacon," said I.

"To be sure!" was his reply; "at the same time allow me the pleasure of introducing you to this young lady friend of mine, Miss Phantasia."

I happened to be in that frame of mind to which one might apply the Horatian *nil mirari*. Nothing of what I saw surprised me, not even the appearance in the flesh of a man like Bacon, who had taken his departure

from our planet some five hundred years ago.
I therefore simply accepted his obliging offer,
and began by asking for an explanation of the
figures and words on the tower.

"On yonder tower, over the clock-face?"
answered he. "Why, that means simply this,
that we have arrived at the first day of the
new year 2071."

"But what is the time? I see so many
hands and figures on the clock, that I am perfectly bewildered."

"What kind of time is it you want to
know?" asked he in reply; "true, mean, or

ALEUTIC TIME?

for each of these has its own set of hands and
figures."

"I know full well," said I, "what *true* time
is, also what is understood by *mean* time, but
what on earth is meant by *aleutic time?*"

"I will soon explain," spoke my obliging
guide. "Since the whole globe has been
encircled by one large net of telegraph lines,

and wire messages,* whether east or westward
bound, do the whole round of our planet in a
single moment, it has been found necessary to
adopt a kind of time that would apply to any
spot of the earth; for by some such contriv-
ance alone was it possible to avoid a confusion
that would have been fatal in many cases,
more especially in those of commercial transactions, when the knowledge of the right time
is an object of no mean consideration. By
mutual agreement the several nations therefore

* At the end of the nineteenth century the Saxon
element had almost entirely disappeared from the
English tongue; even the most intelligible Norman
words had had to give way to the most miraculous
novelties in the shape of bad Greek and Latin
compounds. At the revival of the genuine national
dialect all such abominable mongrels as *telegram,
bicycle, velocipede,* etc., were expelled from decent
conversation. A *telegram* became a *wire-message*; a
bicycle a *two-wheel;* a *velocipede* a *swift-foot; post-
mortem* examinations went by the name of *after-death*
examinations; and as the language gained in nationality, the nation's mind grew in clearness. The change
was a change for the better.   T.

selected the largest of the Aleutic islands, by way of a neutral point or centre. When the sun rises on the east coast of that island, then begins the *world-day*. Nor has the selection of the neutral point been in any way an arbitrary one; for east and west of the meridian which passes over that island are to be found those very latitudes where the confusion of time was formerly at its height; and for this reason, that according to their discovery having been accomplished either from Europe in easterly direction round Africa, or westward round America, *one* whole day had been lost or gained. Now the consequence of this was, that in the islands of these latitudes the inhabitants of the eastern coasts and those dwelling in the west differed four-and-twenty hours in their calculations of time, owing to the circumstance that they belonged to, or were descended from, the one or the other ancient colony. The adoption of an Aleutic time has put a stop to any such confusion."

Having thus endeavoured to satisfy my

curiosity, my companion went on to say: "Do come along with us; we shall have plenty of opportunity to show you other matters of interest in the city of Londinia."

"Londinia? Is that the same as London?"

"Not quite; ancient London formed but a small portion of the present city of Londinia. The latter occupies a considerable part of the south-east of England, and has a population of something like twelve millions."

As we continued our tour, I chanced to hit upon the trivial remark that we had "very mild weather indeed, considering the time of the year."

"You are mistaken," Bacon said; "on the contrary, it is bitterly cold; only you forget that we are in town. Just feel the heat of the current of air which rises from the sieve-like plate on which you are walking, and you will doubtless agree with me that the

DISTRIBUTION-OF-WARM-AIR SOCIETY

is by no means unfaithful to its obligations.

Then look above you. Had the distribution been insufficient, we should still see the glass roof over our heads covered with this morning's snow."

I looked up, and saw that the street was vaulted over with glass plates of considerable length and width, joined together by thin bars, with here and there an aperture as the means of ventilation.

"I apprehend, then, that we are in a so-called arcade?"

"Well, yes; if you mean to apply that name to the greater part of our city. That which in the nineteenth century was only to be found *occasionally* in the great towns of Europe, has become a *regular* institution in the twenty-first, owing to the manufacture of our inexpensive

VERRE SANS FIN,

or 'Endless Glass,' as our people generally call it."

"I have no doubt that this must be a considerable improvement on your town-life throughout winter; but in summer-time I should say this must be intolerably hot."

"Not at all; the same society which undertakes the supply of warm air in winter also provides for us during the summer months a cooling draught. Nothing can be easier than that. You are doubtless aware of ice having been manufactured in the middle of summer for at least a couple of centuries. During the warm season the air is made to pass over the glass vault above us before it reaches the pavement through the sieve-like plate, and if the warm-air inspectors properly attend to their duties, there is scarcely any difference in our temperature throughout the year."

"Then probably you warm your houses by a similar process, and you never use any stoves or fireplaces now?"

Neither of my companions could help smiling at these words, betraying again, as they did, my very old-fashioned notions. Bacon, however, gave me a kindly nod of assent as he proceeded to explain: "Just as a cold-water bath may be heated at pleasure by opening the hot-water tap, we can warm the air in our apartments by means of a valve, which when opened, not only affords a supply of warm air, but has the additional advantage of producing a most delightful refreshing of the atmosphere without any idea of draught."

"I really cannot understand," Miss Phantasia here remarked, "how the people in those barbarous times managed to live amid the smoke and ashes and dust of their horrible fireplaces."

"And then their chimneys on fire," added Bacon; "thank Fate, we have done with that too. Poor insurance offices, they don't pay half the premium now of what they used to do."

"One more question," said I, "before we leave this subject. What do you call the metal used for those elegant little bars which connect and support the roof of glass above us? Surely they are not of iron, as they would have been in my time?"

"No," answered my guide; "iron, on account of its greater specific weight, would have been less suitable here than aluminium; the latter not only corresponds in weight with the glass which it supports, but it also withstands the effects of the atmosphere far better than iron. You will very soon perceive in how many instances the new metal has superseded the old one, in additional proof of which I would just mention the fact that the modern antiquarians do not exclusively now speak of the ages of stone, bronze, and iron, but that they have formally recognised the

AGE OF ALUMINIUM,

The latter commenced or dates from the second half of the twentieth century, when it was first discovered how to produce aluminium in large quantities from common clay, old tiles, potsherds, china, and earthenware."

"Ah!" said I, "here, then, we have another striking example to teach us that discoveries simply arrived at by purely scientific processes searched after from the pure motive of increase of knowledge, may often be ultimately productive of the greatest practical use. The same metal which for years after Wöhler's discovery continued to be a curiosity—so much so that a few grains of it were preserved among the collections of chemical preparations—has now become universally beneficial, nay, a perfect godsend to those districts where clay, *i.e.* aluminium ore, is the only underground wealth."

Following up this idea, at the risk of being ridiculed or, perhaps, reprimanded for my impertinent garrulousness, I continued in the following strain:

"Think of the phosphorus discovered by Brandt and Künckel as early as 1669, yet never getting into common use until the lucifers, fusees, and 'flamers' made their appearance some two hundred years afterwards; and of chloroform, now the greatest alleviation of suffering humanity, although Dumas, when he first compounded it, did but little dream of its application. Then, again, when Sir Humphry

Davy's remarkable experiments taught him the refrigerating power of metal gas, did this not ultimately lead to the invention of the safety lamp? and not only has the latter already preserved thousands of human lives, but, more than that, the principle of Davy's invention has actually become the basis upon which all steam-engines are constructed, as well as those by which ice can be made at any time. With regard to the invention of the art of photography, how could it have become a reality, a possibility, without the number of purely scientific discoveries that preceded it; aye, purely scientific discoveries, such as Porta's so-called *camera obscura* * (sixteenth century); Scheele's discovery of the discoloration of chloride of silver by light, at which he did not arrive until two

---

* The *camera obscura* (dark chamber) is a closed space impervious to light. Porta, the inventor here referred to, was a Neapolitan physician. He found that by fixing a double convex lens in the aperture, and placing a white screen in the focus, the image was much brighter and more definite.   T.

hundred years afterwards; Courtois's finding of the iodine, 1811; or the invention of gun cotton, from which Schönbein learned to make collodion; nor would it be difficult to name several other materials, all found by regular chemical processes, to fix the photographic images, and to make them permanent."

Encouraged by my companion's "line of non-intervention," I ventured to continue to speak my thoughts aloud.

"If any art more than another," said I, "is calculated to illustrate the fact that the most important discoveries—such as have been most universally brought to bear upon the joint social condition of mankind—have simply resulted from the inventions of scientific men who never dreamt of the practical application of their discoveries; if any such thing exists, surely it is the telegraph. Could these magic wires have lurked in the mind of Thales when he found out, now twenty-five centuries ago, that a piece of amber, when rubbed, attracts light bodies, even although it led him to discover the very first of those phenomena, the cause of which must be sought in that mysterious power which now we call electricity? Did Galvani think of the telegraphic art when he noticed how the muscles of his frogs contracted under the influence of electricity?* or Volta, when, following up Galvani's experiments, he produced the pile that bears his name? And yet that was, so to speak, the embryo of those modern batteries of ours whence proceeds the marvellous action along the wire. Nor is it in any way presumable that Oerstedt ever thought of the application of his discovery to telegraphy, when he first noticed that the

---

* Galvani was a professor of anatomy in the university of Bologna. While engaged in his anatomical investigations he observed, accidently so to say, that when the lumbar nerves of a dead frog were connected with the crural muscles by a metallic circuit, the latter became briskly contracted. The electricity theory drawn by Galvani from his observation of the frog was chiefly opposed by the philosopher likewise here mentioned, Alexander Volta, professor of physics in Pavia.   T.

magnetic needle is deflected under the influence of electricity;* no more than Arago, who
found that iron becomes magnetic when an
electric current runs along it through a metal
wire.

"No, no!" cried I; "none of those men
could ever have foreseen the ultimate beneficial
results of these discoveries of natural truths."†

"You are perfectly right in your remarks,"
said Bacon, as I paused. "From my own per-
sonal knowledge of what has come to pass

---

* Oerstedt's discovery, published in the year 1819,
was afterwards considerably extended by Ampère and
Faraday. It laid, however, the foundation of the
recognition by science of the relations between
magnetism and electricity.   T.

† Nor did La Condamine probably suspect that the
small bottle of india-rubber, which he brought with
him on his return from a scientific tour to America,
and passed round as a curiosity to his colleagues of
the French academy, was actually filled with a liquid
destined to become of the most extensive application to
different branches of industry; aye, a liquid without
which the submarine telegraph would simply have
remained an impossibility up to the present day.

in the field of industry during the last two
centuries, I could adduce a good many more
examples to show that many of your nineteenth-century discoveries, which for a long
time afterwards merely bore a purely scientific
significance or character, have now become
prolific sources of material benefit to society
at large.   Nor does any one now-a-days doubt
the importance of pure science; all govern-
ments look upon it as an urgent duty on their
part to promote the same wherever they can ;
nor is it too anxiously asked whether it does
bear, in every instance, immediate results to
benefit the material condition of society. Moreover, it should not be here forgotten that every
man of judgment and discrimination has long
since learned to see that the furtherance of
material advantages as the aim and end of
human endeavours is an idea as narrow in
itself as it is unworthy of rational beings.
Surely there exists another and infinitely
higher mainspring of happiness in the enjoy-
ment of gathering such knowledge as will

enable us to perceive the causal connection between the phenomena of nature, or teach us the history of man and all his surroundings. The pursuit of material gratification is essentially a thing which man shares with the brute; but our desire to ennoble that which is spiritual or immaterial in us—that is exclusively human; the gratification of such desire is the genuine 'trade-mark' of real civilization. So much is the bulk of modern society already convinced of these truths, that no government could now-a-days afford to neglect the encouragement of scientific pursuit, although the utmost discretion be left to the men of science themselves with regard to the other question: how and in what direction the extension of knowledge ought to take place."

"Then you hear nothing more now of what was once termed 'official science'?"

"I really do not know," said Bacon, "what you are alluding to; but if you use the word 'official' in its usual acceptation—meaning that which can no longer be doubted, since it

emanated from a responsible government—
then, my dear sir, you will pardon me the
remark that the expression is anything but
felicitous, nay, very shallow indeed. A
government may protect, support, and promote science, but it can never stamp it with
the seal of genuineness. Such seal is held
by truth alone!"

Somewhat ashamed of my apparently an-
tiquated notions and childish observations, I
walked on in silence until Miss Phantasia all
of a sudden exclaimed: "Here we have actually got to the exhibition of

HELIOCHROMES;

oh, *do* let us go in. I should very much like
to know whether they come at all up to those
enormous golden placards outside, and whether
the highest of the fine arts is here equalled by
reality."

There was something spiteful in the remarks
of the young lady; and at my question of
what was meant by heliochromes, she again

sarcastically replied, "Oh! nothing but photographs in the natural colours of the objects as pencilled by the sun himself; so, at least, in her extravagant style, says my friend Realia." *

"Ha!" exclaimed I, "the ultimate triumph of the life-long endeavours of that plucky Frenchman, De Saint-Victor! final fruits of the *prix* Trémont awarded him by the French Academy!"

Bacon looked at me with a smile clearly indicative of his contempt for my helpless ignorance. But all he said was this: "Come inside, please, and you will have something else to see than those rude and perishable experiments of Victor of the nineteenth century."

We entered, and I could not trust my eyes. The walls of the building were covered with innumerable pictures, landscapes, portraits, and *genre*-pieces, some of the figures life-size; and all these pictures were mere photographs, yet

* Such photographs have been produced in Italy since the third edition of this work appeared in the original text.   T.

photographs differing as much from those that I was familiar with as an oil painting does from a crayon drawing.

"Unhappy artists! poor arts!" I exclaimed; "what have you come to at last?"

But Miss Phantasia appeared to share my delight no more than my sympathy. "Unhappy artists, indeed," was her reply, "if by such honourable name you designate those knights of the brush whose sole aim and end is the faithful imitation of reality; but do not say poor arts! They have by no means died out, the worthy successors of Raphael and Corregio, of Rubens and Rembrandt, of those whose calling was not to imitate nature, but to idealise it. And that is the vocation of art. Simple imitation is mere handicraft. And although the monuments and statues of living persons *are* now mechanically taken from photographs, aye, by a common workman who has no notion of art; yet have we sculptors who are genuine artists, creators of the ideal."

I quietly accepted the rebuff, and rejoiced to think that all those treasures of art of which my country is so proud had not then, after all, deteriorated in worth; on the other hand, it was to me a matter of little moment that mediocre talents, incapable of rising above the imitation of reality, had been compelled to exchange the brush for the *camera obscura;* and I had no doubt that their productions would thereby gain—in faithfulness.

As we left the exhibition building, I saw a huge waggon without any horses, but simply governed by one man, in spite of which it seemed to roll on as easily as possible, and to pull up at pleasure. The waggon was loaded with all sizes of black-coloured cylinders, resembling casks or barrels. I was perfectly aware of the numerous successful experiments made long ago in England and elsewhere with the construction of steam-engines destined to run, not along iron rails, but along the ordinary roads. I could not, however, help noticing that this waggon differed totally from those old locomobiles, inasmuch as there were no signs of steam about the novelty.

Once more I turned to my amiable guide for an explanation; but although he immediately prepared to comply with my request, still I am obliged to confess that not everything was quite clear to me. I imagine this was partly owing to Bacon's making use of the names of engines and materials with which I was unfamiliar; but this is about what I understood him to say:

"So long as we had abundance of coal, the use of steam was found to be amply sufficient for the locomotion of all kinds of engines, waggons, or carriages; but about the beginning of this century the quantity of coal in the different countries of Europe had decreased to such an extent that the price of the article became by far too high for daily and ordinary use. True, the supply of North America was far from being exhausted; but, of course, the exportation from thence could not but influence the cost. The same inconvenience further presented itself with such engines where the locomotive power was produced by continually recurring explosions of a mixture of light-gas and common atmospheric air, since the cost of light-gas naturally increased with the decrease of coal, from which it was principally made. Under these circumstances, recourse was had to the electro-magnetic machines, which could not be used to advantage so long as coals were inexpensive; now, however, these were not only able to compete with the different kinds of steam-engines, but they had this advantage over the latter, that they were entirely free from the danger of explosive boilers.

"Nevertheless the electro-magnetic power, with all its improvements, was, and remained, a more expensive one than that formerly produced through coal, and the consequence of this was a decrease in the produce of a great many things which had not only grown into matters of daily necessity, but even into a *sine quâ non* of a progressive and lasting civilization.

Then it was, since necessity is the mother of invention, that every one contrived to devise a new means of locomotion, until, after innumerable unsuccessful experiments, a power was finally arrived at in every way practical and satisfactory, whilst inexhaustible in its sources. It was, namely, this.

From time immemorial people knew the two motive forces of flowing water and of streaming air, or wind. When the steam-engines came into use, the latter had gradually superseded the former, partly because rapidly flowing or falling water is not always procurable, partly also because the supply of water, as well as its power, depends on the quantities of rain falling in the higher districts. The latter inconvenience, the variability of power, made itself still more strongly felt in the application of the wind. The most absolute quietness in the air may be followed by tempests so danger-ous that the skipper is obliged to furl his sails, and the miller finds it necessary to stop his mill, in order to avoid the most disastrous consequences. Now, when the mill stops, it becomes a useless machine; for then the work of the men is stopped, and ultimately their wages. Much valuable time is lost, and time is known to be money. Add to this that a steam-engine may be worked unremittingly, so that the manufacturer can be sure to finish any given work in any stipulated time, and it must be clear enough why the powers of water and wind got to be superseded by steam-power, on account of the latter's superior regularity.

"Meanwhile it is impossible to overlook the double fact that water and wind may be had for nothing, and that steam involves expense. Moreover, so immense is the quantity of vital or working power of the water falling down on the surface of our earth, and also of the atmospheric currents, that the locomotive power of all existing steam-engines is comparatively trifling by the side of them. One single great cataract has more working power than all the steam-engines of Europe together, and one single thunder-storm may produce such frightful destruction that it would be ridiculous to measure them by horse-power.

" As, therefore, steam became more and more expensive, one naturally looked for means by which, without losing the regularity and stability of steam-power, one might turn to account the forces of wind and falling water. The question had really come to this—how to regularly distribute over a certain period of time a force or power so intensely variable. It seemed as if the working-power of water and wind had to be collected and saved up, so as to have a regular provision of such forces in case of need. In like manner Nature had saved her working-power when she caused the forests to grow, from whence resulted the coal layers. Art had already done the same in preparing gunpowder and other explosive matters. Why, then, could the experiment not be tried in analogous form, namely, by temporary imprisonment or detention of that vital power which appeared to be so inexhaustible?"

That was the problem. With regard to its

solution I could not well follow the details. All I could learn from Bacon was this, that the black cylinders on the waggon already referred to bore the name of

ENERGEIATHECS,

force-holders, or energy-preservers; that one of these set the waggon in motion, whilst the others were to be delivered either at private houses for domestic purposes of hoisting, raising, or carrying; or to blacksmiths, turners, and other artisans, who wanted motive powers not so extensive as regular. Large manufactories used similar energeiathecs, only of greater power and dimensions. Some of these (in mountainous districts) collected the power of falling water; others (situated in the lower districts) utilised the wind.

With regard to the construction, etc., of those cylinders, I could do nothing more than to form a faint idea. Thus I thought of compressed air, or some other gas, which, by some strong pressure or other might have been turned into a liquid or hard substance retaining the capability of rendering again its deposit of force on subsequent explosion. But I merely give this hypothesis for what it is worth.

While Bacon had thus been endeavouring to enlighten me on a subject which after all I did not profess to understand, we had reached the aluminium railings of an elegant and lofty edifice, bearing the inscription,

NATIONAL LIBRARY.

Naturally enough, I evinced a strong desire to enter, but Bacon remarked that a visit to such a place would take up a good deal of valuable time, that might be turned to a much more pleasurable and profitable account; to which Miss Phantasia added that if the gentlemen chose to enter that labyrinth of learning, she, for her part, preferred a walk in the square; the latter, crossed in all directions by parks and avenues and flower-beds, was moreover crowded with the most exquisite works of ancient and modern sculptors, living illustrations of her former assertion that genuine works of art had not quite died out.

As soon as we had arrived at the opposite side of the square, I fully understood the wisdom of Bacon's remarks. So far as my eyes reached, I could see a dense cluster of buildings, more resembling a moderately sized town than a depository of literature. "You see, my friend," Bacon said, "it is imperative here to make up your mind what to see, or else our lady friend will be tired of waiting. Which branch of human knowledge do you give the preference to?"

I answered that I was especially interested in works of natural science.

"Impossible to think of visiting the buildings in which all these are deposited. You will have to restrict yourself considerably."

"Well, then, let us confine ourselves to zoology."

"Too much even for the most cursory glance. It would take us hours to have a mere walk through. Select a sub-section of zoology."

"Shall we say the literature of entomology?"

"That won't do either; you must keep to one single order of insects."

"Well, then, be good enough to select for yourself," said I ; " I'll follow you."

We entered one of the buildings. How I was surprised to see the crowd of officers and attendants ! some anxious to direct and assist the still greater mass of visitors ; others busily engaged in making out tickets and extracts for those scholars who had not time enough to do any such manual work themselves. I felt that this was an admirable school for young students, who were here able not only to gather a valuable knowledge of books, but also to form themselves into independent thinkers and writers.

NINETEENTH-CENTURY BOOKS.

As I looked round, I saw one of the junior attendants engaged in gumming the leaves of a musty book on sheets of collodion, so that one side of the leaf remained at least legible. I remembered that this was the way in which the papyrus scrolls of Pompeii and Herculaneum were preserved from utter destruction; but how great was my astonishment to see that the title-page of the musty book bore the year mark 1860, Amsterdam. "So it is with most of the nineteenth-century books," said Bacon. "Owing to the bleaching properties of chlorine, the paper on which they have been printed got so thin, and mouldy, and worm-eaten, that we have but few works of those days now left; and that is really to be regretted, for many writings of that time were quite worth preserving."

I must confess that I was sorry to hear this little bit of information, so distressing to an author of that age; but, of course, I was silent, and kept on following my guide through rows and rows of apartments, until we arrived at last at a vast hall, literally crammed with books from top to bottom. There we paused,

and Bacon turned round to address me. " Now
we are among the literature of the two-winged
insects; what work do you wish to see ?" But
staring at those thousands of volumes of
treatises on gnats and flies, I was too much
afraid again to betray my ignorance; I felt
sure I would hit upon some title or other to
convince my guide how little I was *au courant*
of the twenty-first century.   I limited myself
to expressing my gratification at what I had
already seen, and added that I would not
trespass any further upon the obliging courtesy
of my friend.

   And thus we left the National Library, an
institution which they might safely have called
the *bibliopolis*, for indeed it was like a *city of
books.*

   As we passed once more through the front
gate on our return, we came across a crowd of
men who were about to enter, and whom I
judged by their dress and appearance to
belong to the class of artizans. I asked Bacon
what business had those people there ?

"These are workmen from a neighbouring factory," answered he; "they come here in turns for an hour every day, in order to read in yonder room, especially set apart for them, such books as the library committee has judged to be adapted to their wants. Such workmen's libraries exist in all the several quarters of the city, but they are most numerous in the densely populated districts where most factories are to be found."

"And are they well frequented? And do employers allow their workmen to make use of them? And have they reduced their wages in consequence? Are they not afraid that their men will thus become too clever, too well educated?"

"With regard to your first two questions—yes; with regard to the latter two—no. So far as employers are concerned, they have long been taught by experience that, by allowing their *employés* one hour's relaxation daily, they act in their own interest; that is to say, when such an hour's "holiday" be turned to good

account by the men themselves, by learning
something more about their business, and con-
tributing to their mental development generally. Besides, what else could have happened,
since the continual invention of new machinery has done away with so much of our
manual labour?   Naturally enough, a greater
demand has set in among the working classes
for knowledge and intellectual culture, and
this has shown itself in the same proportion
as the demand for mere handicraft has sub-
sided."

"Pity, though," said I, "for those who
cannot make use of the library."

"*Cannot !*" exclaimed my guide; "but the
doors are open to every one."

"Except to those who are unable to read, I
suppose."

"Unable to read !" retorted Bacon; "but we
are in Europe, my dear sir, not among the
Hottentots or Bushmen!   There is not one
man or woman amongst us but what can read
and write, and even do some arithmetic.

Surely these elements of knowledge are the very first steps on the field of culture, and the *sine quâ non* of a person's being a useful member of society."

"Do I then understand from your remarks that you have arrived at last at a system of

COMPULSORY EDUCATION?"

"Most decidedly, sir! How could you doubt that for a moment? If parents are obliged to maintain their children with food and the 'necessaries of life,' why should they not be compelled to look after the nurturing of their minds?"

"Why, because the one is a moral obligation, whereas, if I rightly understand you, school education has been made compulsory by the law; and this would appear to me to be an infringement of individual liberty, and of the rights of parents."

"You did understand me rightly, so far as the law is concerned; but permit me, sir, to point out to you that you have taken a very

one-sided view of the question of compulsion.
You will probably admit that for any properly
managed society to exist, every member of the
same has to sacrifice a portion of his individual
liberty in the interests of the whole of which
he forms part.   In many cases such sacrifices
are borne without any reluctance or opposition;
then, namely, when they are visibly and
amply compensated by the many advantages
involved in our living in a well-regulated
society.   With regard to the much-vaunted
rights of parents, it should never be lost sight
of that the children have their rights as well;
aye, from the moment they enter upon this
world; and one of these rights is that they,
born in civilized society, where ignorance is
excluded as a foreign element, must be somehow enabled to appropriate some culture to
themselves.   If now the parents abuse their
rights *by sheer force* it becomes the duty of
the state to intervene on behalf of the weaker,
and, by legal exactions, protect the children in
their future welfare.   This is, at the same

time, in the interests of the state; for the experience of preceding centuries, when compulsory education was not universally recognised, has taught us again and again that the jails of Europe were mostly filled with those that could neither read nor write."

"One more question permit me. Has not the introduction of compulsory education been accompanied by great, almost insuperable obstacles ?"

" That these obstacles were at least not *insuperable* you may easily gather from the fact that, even in the nineteenth century, the compulsory measure existed in some parts of Germany, and met with no opposition. Of course, on its application to other countries, some difficulties had at first to be surmounted; for all novelties meet with opposition somewhere, and all changes are fraught with more or less evil somehow. At first the measure had to be occasionally enforced by the arm of the law, but a very few years sufficed for the legal clause to grow into a popular habit; and the present generation, grown up under its beneficent influence, is so deeply convinced of the indispensability of some elementary knowledge in every member of society, that the law might be safely repealed without fear that any school would lose a single pupil."*

Bacon's arguments were by no means lost upon me; nay, it seemed now almost strange and inexplicable to me that in an age when the word "progress" proceeded and was re-echoed from lip to lip, so absolute a *sine quâ non* of progress could have found opponents. But then I remembered at the same time that the word progress admitted of more accepta-

---

* The truth of this remark cannot, I think, be sufficiently impressed upon the even now existing opposition minority in England. Let us have compulsory education for three, or even two, generations, and every citizen in the state will be so well educated himself as to know the value of education, and not to deny it his children. The repeal of any law, prohibitory or compulsory, can only prove this, that the people for whom the measure was originally framed have *risen* in the scale of moral and social organization.

T.

tions than one. I was about to inquire of Bacon in what sense the term was taken in the twenty-first century, when my eye fell upon another row of buildings far greater in extent than those constituting the National Library. I was informed by my guide that we had arrived at the National Museum. "Here," said he, "are preserved some glorious works of art and all the most remarkable objects of nature."

"I easily understand," said I, "that even the ordinary tourist would require a couple of days to gratify his morbid curiosity in this *enceinte;* but could I not see some small department at least of all these sightworthy productions?"

"Well," answered Miss Phantasia, "let us see the collection in the

GENEALOGICAL MUSEUM;

that is my hobby," continued she, as she stopped before one of the edifices.

Could I trust my ears! A young lady's favourite study was genealogy; old parchments, coats-of-arms, and heraldry her hobbies! However, I could but follow her, and as I did so, and arrived at our destination, I saw none of her "hobbies" at all; from one single centre, spreading into innumerable directions and ramifications, I observed a collection of skeletons; several of them were indeed old acquaintances, such as the elephant, the mammoth, the mastodont, the rhinoceros, the horse, the hippotherium, the anchitherium, the palaeotherium, the lophiodon, etc., etc.; but a far greater number apparently represented the remains of creatures altogether unknown to me; they were arranged, not only according to their general dates of discovery, but also on the basis of organic relationship, so that those forms nearest to each other showed the nearest approach in outward appearance, whereas the extreme forms on both sides bore the most astonishing contrast.

It now became clear to me in what sense our fair companion had used the qualification of genealogical, not as referring to the noble trees of families but to indicate the various ways by which the animal species that have at one time lived on this earth had developed one from the other. Miss Phantasia appeared to attach great value to this genealogical collection; but still I could not help remarking to her that this process of exhibiting the fossils of animal species did by no means prove what it was intended to do; "for," said I, "up to the present day there are to be found *on our globe, and alive*, all sorts of mutually related forms and intermediate varieties.

· "Ah, well!" exclaimed the bright-eyed, lively damsel, "you would think differently if you were acquainted with all the new discoveries of our age."*

---

* Like the ingenious author of the "Origin of Species," Miss Phantasia appears to have convinced herself that the time would come when the absence or rarity of intermediate species, *the* great stumbling-block in the grand Darwinian theory, would no longer have to be accounted for *negatively* by the "poorness of our palæontalogical collections," and the "imperfectness of the genealogical record." Bacon, though apparently familiar with, and not averse to, Mr.

Perfectly agreeing with Miss Phantasia, so far as my ignorance went, I thought I had better drop the subject altogether; still I ventured to ask her one more question : Did this museum at the same time contain the ancestors of the human race ? In reply she pointed to a row of veiled figures in the background of the hall; but as she took my hand to conduct me thither, Bacon stepped between us, and said, " Let not my fair friend tempt you ; you would not be able to see anything in that dark corner over there; the evening is falling. Go you to your hotel; we too are homeward bound."

Indeed, the evening *was* falling, but only in the building; for as soon as we got outside, we found ourselves apparently in broad daylight. I looked about me for gas-flames and lamp-posts, but I could discover nothing of the kind.

Darwin's theory of evolution, does not seem to follow the doctrine out in its application to the human race. How many errors remain to be eradicated, even in minds of the highest order, through man's adopted notion that he stands exclusively apart from all his natural surroundings, both in degree *and in kind !*

T.

At last I looked up to the sky, and then I saw
far above the houses a dazzling light, somewhat like the sun, spreading his rays in all
directions, and several more of these " suns "
at considerable distances from one another.

" Don't you even know the

SOLAR LIGHT ? "

Bacon asked.   " That surprises me; for as far
back as the second half of the nineteenth century it was used to illuminate both here and
in Paris some of the public edifices.   Here it
has been generally introduced for some time
past, ever since the streets have been covered
with our endless glass."

" But then that light is too brilliant and too
white; that can't be gas-light."

" Nor is it.   Gas is now only burnt in those
isolated districts where the houses stand far
apart from each other, but the central part of
the city is chiefly lighted up by the burning
of magnesium, and sometimes also by electric
light, or any of the numerous lights with

which we are now acquainted. The apparatus, consisting of mirrors and lenses, to collect the light and to make the beams parallel, *i.e.* equal to sunlight, is the same for all those different kinds of public illumination."

" Rather expensive, though," was my sudden reply.

" Not as expensive as you think," continued Bacon; "especially not in the case of magnesium, for there is an abundance of magnesium ore in the form of dolemite, etc., from which we get the metal in a way as inexpensive as that followed in the preparation of aluminium. To this must be added that the process of burning this metal yields a hard substance, which, by a suitable arrangement of the apparatus, can be collected again and re-reduced to magnesium. Speaking theoretically, a certain quantity of magnesium is a source of light quite as inexhaustible as the oil-jar of the widow of Sarepta of which we read in the Book of Kings."

The more I looked about, the more I arrived

at the humiliating conclusion that we of the boasting nineteenth century—of which I still felt to be a child—were really very much benighted, and I could almost forgive Miss Phantasia for speaking of the semi-barbarous condition of society in my time.

It seemed as if Bacon read my thoughts by my features; for he continued as follows: "I see that you are desirous of increasing your acquaintance with the present state of affairs. Well, then, if you have been able to put up with our company to-day, you had better join us to-morrow, in our contemplated aërial voyage."

How I thrilled with inward delight at the prospect of such a tour! Of course I accepted the kind offer without hesitation, although I could not help raising a slight point of doubt with regard to the state of the weather.

"Don't you trouble your mind about that," said my amiable guide; "early this morning I was at the meteorological institute, and I have ascertained that the weather will be fine for a fortnight at all events. The reports from the different meteorological stations are all equally propitious. The sky will be bright, and the wind favourable; I should be surprised if the aëronaut would have any occasion to use the energeiathecs, which, however, will accompany us as preventatives."

We parted company, but not until I had made a note of the spot where it was intended we should meet on the following morning. I hailed one of the numerous cabs on the stand, and ordered the driver to take me to my hotel. As I drove on, I was agreeably surprised not to hear anything of that rattling noise over the pavement, which is alike obnoxious to the person inside the vehicle, to all the passers-by, and to the inmates of houses situated in public thoroughfares. I heard nothing, indeed, but the melodious tinkling of four little bells tied round the horse's neck, and forming a musical chord. I am sorry to say that I was not fortunate enough to discover whether this "gentle process" was attributable to the nature of the pavement, or to certain hoops (not iron ones) round the wheels.   Probably it was the one as much as the other.

THE TELEPHON.

Arrived at my hotel, I was at once struck with its extreme quietness, more so as the apartments were all but taken by some thousands of travellers.   The cause of this, however, I soon discovered on entering the elegant and spacious conversation room.   Methought I heard a kind of music, feeble, yet melodious in the extreme.   The sound approached as near as possible that of the human voice; but still the quality was altogether different.   Besides, no artist, male or female, was to be seen in the room.   The only cue that I could get to the mystery was through a box of small dimensions; this instrument was placed on a table right in the centre of the room, and thence the sound appeared to proceed. Taking the affair to be an ordinary musical-box, worked in the usual way, I gazed with no little contempt and surprise upon the crowd of serious-looking, enthusiastic men and women who had clustered round the table. As soon as the music ceased, I ventured to approach the spectators, at the same time asking one among the crowd for some information with regard to the musical instrument in which they all seemed to be so much interested.

Oh the number of pairs of eyes that stared at me, full of amazement, if not of indignation! At last one of the enthusiasts condescended to break the silence, "What, sir, a musical *instrument!* where did you ever know such tones to proceed from a musical *instrument?* Surely, sir, as a gentleman you must have heard of the telephon?"

I now remembered that a machine bearing that name, and answering that description, had been invented as far back as 1861 by a certain Reis; also that it was based upon the following law, as discovered and laid down by Page; namely, that when an electric current passes through a wire coiled round an iron bar, and the current is continually interrupted, there arises a sound or a tone, the height or depth of which is entirely dependent on the number of vibrations produced by the interruptions of the current, according to their succeeding each other with more or less velocity. This recurring to my mind, I now replied that the telephon was indeed not quite unfamiliar to me, in proof of which I went back to the history of its first invention; I also gave a description of Reis' little instrument, by which the sound of the human voice could be transmitted through very great distances; and finally, I added my surmise or natural conviction that such an instrument must have been considerably improved upon in the course of more than two centuries.* I was happy

---

* It is but fair to say that the apparatus of Léon Scott for registering the vibrations produced by the voice in singing had preceded the discovery of Reis. Scott's "phonautograph" is fully described, both in construction and working, in Ganot's Treatise on Physics (Atkinson's translation, p. 211, etc.)　　T.

to notice the excellent impression visibly produced by my words; there now arose a
tolerably general murmur of "whoever now
would have taken the telephon to be so old an
affair?" As for me, I was complimented on
my antiquarian knowledge, and, thanks to the
amiable disposition of the visitors towards
me, I was not long in discovering what had
been going on. That which every one now
was so anxious to explain to me amounted, in
a few words, to this. The North-American
papers had of late been indulging in the most
extravagant terms of praise with regard to a
lady singer who, according to the Yankee cri-
tics, was possessed of a voice such as no mortal
had ever yet heard of, surpassing in compass
and quality everything that could be imagined;
a talent whereby all the artists of former ages
—if history could be relied on—ladies like
Catalani, Malibran, Henriette Sonntag, Jenny
Lind, or the Pattis, were really no more in
comparison than a cricket to a nightingale.

Of course, as might be imagined, these

reports from across the Atlantic had created
an immense stir in the musical world of Londinia. From all directions the managers of
concerts and operas had been induced to nego-
tiate with this marvellous talent, so that it
should no longer be hidden from the musical
inhabitants of Londinia. But, then, all these
reports emanated from the States, the *fons et
origo* of humbug; and, probably taught by experience, the managers had all clubbed together,
and, at their joint expense, despatched a telegram to the gifted artist, requesting her to allow
her marvellous power to be tested by means of
the telephon. That would, at all events, enable
them to judge of the compass and quality of
her voice. To this the lady had consented,
and thereupon the managers had hired one of
the transatlantic telegraph cables, on which
the experiment had been made.

As a clear indication of the compass of the
voice, I was shown sundry slips of black paper
on which could be seen numerous curved white
lines; the latter had been traced upon the paper

by the phonautographer standing behind the telephon, and were supposed to mark the musical scales within compass of the lady's voice. An impression of these slips of paper was to appear, on the following morning, in the musical journal, *Panharmonia*, in order that "the eyes of the inhabitants of Londinia might anticipate the glorious treat in store for the musical ears of the great metropolis." "For," added the editor of the *Panharmonia*, "all connoisseurs in music know the meaning of these little waves. Won't they be astonished when they see a tone like this!" Saying this, he pointed with his finger to the very extreme line where the little curves met as near as possible.

Of course I was longing to examine the construction of the telephon. I was just about to ask one of the gentlemen present to give me some explanation on the subject, when there was a general demand for silence. The American lady was to afford us another treat. This time she sang an air from Mozart's Don Giovanni, and I was delighted to find that this

masterpiece of the great *maestro* was not forgotten even three centuries after the composer's
death.

At the close of her examination, the lady
was unanimously declared worthy to appear
before the critical public of Londinia, and she
received what we might term a musical ovation
by means of another telephon working in
opposite direction. And here the matter was
allowed to rest, it being left to the different
managers to endeavour to engage her services.
All and each of these gentlemen looked as if
they were in possession of some secret or other
wherewith to outvie their competitors. They
parted, however, on the best of terms, and I
retired to my room.

The following morning I was down very
early, and, having enjoyed my breakfast, I
walked slowly towards the place where I expected to meet my companions of the preceding
day. No guide was required in this apparently
immense labyrinth, for nothing indeed was
easier than to find one's way. All the streets,

squares, etc., were namely marked, not by
names as formerly, but by a particular set of
figures, which, with the assistance of a map,
directed me to any given spot; all that was
required to know was two figures, indicating
the point of destination pretty much as with
the latitude and longitude at sea.

I was still at a considerable distance away
from it when I caught sight of a vast building,
on which I read an inscription in gigantic
characters:

GENERAL BALLOON COMPANY.

I had expected to find our starting-point
in some open space, or at least in one of the
squares, and was therefore not a little surprised
to see that this building was situated in one of
the most densely populated neighbourhoods.
Perhaps, thought I, this is merely the office
where the tickets have to be taken. But
when I got nearer, I perceived that the building
differed essentially from other houses in this
respect, that it had an entirely flat roof, which

contained a kind of conveyance, not unlike a ship, but the precise outline of which I could not discover, owing to the glass vault over the street.

Bacon and Miss Phantasia were already on the spot, and after the customary morning greetings we entered to secure our seats. The first thing now was to be weighed; for the price of the passage naturally depended on the volumen of our bodily organization. It need not be said that the young lady came off cheapest. We then passed through a door into a small parlour, or waiting-room, where we found a few more passengers. In the centre of the room I noticed a staircase, and up at the ceiling a kind of trap. Against the walls were several cushioned seats, as in a first-class railway carriage. After a short time the whole apartment seemed to move. I heard a gentle rustling along the walls, as if something were sliding down the paper-hangings. But even before I had time to think on the subject there was a lowering of the trap in the ceiling, and a cheerful greeting of "Welcome a-high, ladies and gentlemen!"

We got upstairs through the aperture, and found ourselves on the flat roof of the building, but precisely underneath the air-ship; we entered, however, the open trap constructed in the latter, for we soon found out that the weather was bitterly cold. This, unfortunately, prevented me from becoming more intimately acquainted with the outward appearance of the balloon, and with its locomotive powers. On the other hand, ample opportunity was afforded us for examining its internal arrangements. As soon as we came into what I can but term the "hold" of the vessel, Bacon called my attention to a long narrow cylinder which ran across the whole length of the ship. "Therein lies," said he, "the whole secret of aëronautics. In order that I may explain this to you, I must remind you of this, that it was formerly impossible to steer any balloon except before the wind. An ordinary vessel, when the keel cuts through the water, can sail half or quarter-wind, because she moves in the two intermediate matters of air and water, the latter offering a greater resistance than the former, and thereby supporting the vessel in her movements; to which must be added that the resistance operates in a definite direction, namely, in that of the motion of the ship, so that by supplying the craft with a rudder or helm one is able to turn her at pleasure to the right or the left.

"But," continued Bacon, "this becomes quite a different matter when a vessel is merely surrounded by air. Driven onward by the wind, which means carried along by the atmospheric current, she meets with no resistance, and therefore lacks every point of support whereby to turn herself. She will always offer the largest of her sides to the wind, which falls upon it at right angles, just the same as on a light piece of paper or cloth whirled round by the wind.

"In order, then, to render such balloon voyages possible at all, it was necessary, in the first place, to afford the machine its required support, its resistance, and this was accomplished in the following manner: The long cylinder which runs along the whole of the ship is a bar of malleable iron, surrounded by a spiral copper wire which has been coated with an insulating substance. If, now, a voltaic current is made to pass along that wire, the bar becomes a most powerful electro-magnet, which, when free in its movements, like the needle of a compass, adopts a direction from south to north, with a slight easterly deviation, and also a certain inclination. When driven out of its natural direction by another power, the needle will endeavour to resume its original inclination. As, now, the magnet and the vessel are so joined together as virtually to form but one body, the balloon, or rather the ship, is in itself a gigantic compass. The inclination is removed just the same as with the needle of the compass. One has merely to alter the centre of gravity, and this can be done in several ways. Thus, all that remains is the direction in the magnetic meridian.

"If, now, the wind blows in the same direction that one wishes to travel, then the apparatus is not worked; that is to say, no current is passed through the wire. Should the wind, however, be unpropitious, then the ship is at once changed into a magnet. For example, suppose the wind to be due west, and the sails to be placed at right angles with the wind, then the vessel will be driven neither east nor northward, but towards a point intermediate; just as a vessel at sea when pushed north by the current of the water, and westward by the wind, does not follow either of these directions exclusively, but an intermediate one. It is not difficult, therefore, to perceive that the aëronaut, by the proper joint working of his sails and of the electro-magnetic apparatus, is enabled to turn his ship into any direction he chooses. Nor is that all. The apparatus also serves as a helm or rudder; for as soon as I press this knob the current is at once reversed; the north pole becomes the south pole, and *vice versâ*. It stands to reason that the vessel must turn under the circumstances, and, of course, according to pleasure; for at any moment the helmsman may interrupt the current, whereby the ship ceases to be a magnet.

"Now, as indeed at sea, the case may be that the wind is too strong, and the power of the magnet insufficient to properly govern the airship. In that case we have recourse to those energeiathecs of which I spoke yesterday; these tend to set in circular motion the four-winged screws which you see here and there peeping out of the sides, and this is always done as near as possible at right angles with the direction in which the vessel has a tendency to deviate.

"Thus it is usually possible to keep the ship in the direction required; but should the aëronaut fail in his attempt to do so, even then he has another resource left him which the seaman lacks. He rises or descends with his air-ship in search of a more favourable wind; nor does he do so at hap-hazard, for

the meteorological institute has long since issued charts upon which are marked the directions of all the air-currents that will probably
be found at any given altitude for any given
time. These charts are arranged in the same
manner as those formerly published by the
institute, which, however, merely showed the
probable direction of the wind in the immediate
vicinity of the earth's surface.

"With regard to the modes of ascent and
descent, they differ somewhat according to
the nature of the various apparatuses, and for
these, to explain them to you in detail—by
which alone you would understand the differ-
ences—we should have to go on deck, and it
is so bitterly cold there, that we are better
where we are. Suffice it to say that the old
clumsy process of throwing out ballast for the
purpose of rising has long been dispensed
with, since it was found that the measure
was merely a partial or momentary one, and
slightly unacceptable to the denizens of the
earth below. The most appropriate method

5

we have learned from nature; it consists, namely, of an imitation of the operation of the swim-bladder in fishes. The latter accomplish their ascent and descent in the water by a greater or lesser compression of that bladder, or of the air contained in it; some of them having even special compression apparatuses for that object. From this you will easily conclude the application of the aquatic locomotion to that of the navigation in the air."

This, I must confess, I did not quite see; but many other points in Bacon's explanation remained to be cleared up. Not a few questions were on the tip of my tongue, but I asked no more. I felt that I was a child of the nineteenth century, too little *au courant* of the science of modern times to understand all that had been accomplished during the last two hundred years; moreover, I feared that by putting more silly questions I should lower myself in the estimation of my friend.

TRAVELLING DIALECT.

Miss Phantasia was of too mercurial a temperament to listen to lengthy descriptions; she had already ascended the steps that led to the saloon, and we now followed her. The compartment looked neat enough, though not comfortable. Everything pointed to the endeavours of rendering all the furniture as light as possible, and this, of course, applied to the whole affair whenever it did not interfere with the necessary solidity. Bamboo canes cut thin and twisted together appeared to be the chief material, and of the metals aluminium was the only one to be seen.

On our entering the waiting-room, I had already noticed that all the passengers conversed with one another in the same tongue, in a dialect of which I certainly recognised a word or two, but yet a foreign idiom to me. On asking my companion what countrymen those gentlemen were, I received the following reply:

"They belong to all sorts of nations. That burly-looking gentleman yonder is a Russian; that ridiculous little man playing with his moustache and ogling all the ladies can only be a Frenchman; the other trunculant figure, who has paid the highest fare, is one of your own countrymen—a Dutchman; those two blue-eyed, flaxen-haired youngsters are Germans, and all the rest are English."

"But how, then, is it that they all speak the same language?"

"They speak the travelling dialect. In our modern days, when many people spend the greater portion of their time in travelling, and all nationalities continually mingle together, such an idiom was created almost spontaneously. True, it is as yet but a language in its infancy; but it will probably, at no great distance of time, become the universal tongue."

I listened as attentively as I dared and could, and I observed very soon that the so-called travelling dialect was a mixture of various tongues, English though preponderating;

and this I ascribed to the fact of the majority of the travelling public being generally Englishmen.

No more War!

As I looked about me, it so happened that my eye fell upon some wide tubes peeping out from the sides and the hold of the vessel. I first thought that these were a new kind of cannon; so I asked whether we were on board of a man-of-war? Miss Phantasia smiled, but her smile was a bitter one immediately followed by a sigh. "War!" she echoed, "those chivalrous times we only know from history; our modern men are manufacturers, merchants, engineers, scholars, legislators, and so forth; but as for soldiers—well, you may see them on the stage occasionally, but our numerous force of constables is the only approach to soldiery we have."

"Is it possible?" cried I; "no more war, and no more standing armies! At last then the idea has triumphed of the peace-men, Cobden,

Bright, and their followers; at last the present
generation has acknowledged that war was an
eternal disgrace to humanity, reducing reason-
ing men to the level of the unreasoning brute,
and causing them to destroy each other's lives
in the blindest fury, instead, alas! of dwelling
together on this beautiful earth in unity, peace,
and concord, for the promotion of mutual happiness!"

"I doubt very much indeed," muttered
Bacon in his teeth, "whether any such con-
siderations as those have brought about the
reign of peace. Mankind, my dear sir, is still
swayed by passion; quite as much, I venture
to say, as in bygone days. Men still deserve
the epithet once served upon them by a foreign
poet: 'angel half, half brute!' and so it will
be in the future, although it can never be
denied that society, as a whole, progresses in a
moral sense. But for this, that 'circumstances
alter cases,' I am afraid there would be war
still. Only circumstances *are* altered, and war
has become an impossibility.

"In the first place, our present condition of peace has been chiefly brought about by the universal state-bankruptcy at the close of the nineteenth century, when the combined debts of the would-be civilised nations (in consequence of the immense expense involved in the large standing armies) had become to surpass the joint national capitals.

"In the second place, the present state of affairs is due to the marvellous improvements lately [made in the weapons of attack and defence.

" When, in the last war, now about a century ago, the navies of England, France, Russia, and America had mutually destroyed one another; when, through a bombardment from both sides of the channel, the capitals of England and France had simultaneously been set on fire ; when the losses on both sides had become incalculable, not to say irreparable, then, but not until then, people began to ask themselves whether even a victory was worth such enormous sacrifices. And it finally dawned in the public mind that *in all wars the conqueror is likewise the loser.*

" But that which has mainly contributed to render war gradually a matter of rare occurrence, and which, we trust, will ultimately lead to its complete abolition, is the vastly increased intercourse between the peoples of various nationalities, by which all those silly inherited national antipathies have slowly become absorbed ; then again, we have had the application of the principles of free trade, the removal of all those barriers that separated nations from nations, an universal system of coinage and weights and measures, an increase in the means of locomotion and communication, and the fusion of the individual interests of particular nations into one great universal ' public weal.' Nations have ceased to stand opposite, against one another, they flourish side by side ; by thousands and thousands of bonds they are joined and held together ; and if the nineteenth century has witnessed the introduction of the principle of nationality, ours has made another step in the right direction, and produced the recognition of the principle of humanism." *

FREE TRADE; UNIVERSAL LOCOMOTION.

I was much impressed with the justness of the last words of my companion. It now became clear to me how every new railroad, every new telegraph line, the removal of every obstacle in the process of exportation and importation, does not only directly promote the general interest and welfare, but that they are

---

* It is embarrassing to render the original German coinage *humanität*, which, we believe, is due to the grand idea of Lessing, but it is a decided fallacy, current even among literati, that the absence of a certain word in a certain language indicates the absence of the idea embodied in the word among the nations by whom that language is spoken. This vulgar error, the prolific source of so many idle boasts, and unjust charges, and national vanities, we have endeavoured to refute in a paper on "The Philosophy of Verbal Monopoly," printed in the "Transactions of the Devonshire Association for the Advancement of Art, Science, and Literature," 1868.

T.

as many links in the great chain by which men are united together in brotherhood as members of one and the same household. And yet methought I perceived a threatening cloud at this bright horizon. "If then," said I, "all wars have ceased to be, and if in consequence thereof, as well as through other propitious circumstances of various kinds, commerce and industry have been constantly progressing, surely you must have witnessed an alarming increase of population; and the production of the necessary food can hardly have kept pace with its consumption."

"If you suppose that we have now, as formerly, many indigent people and others occasionally starving in some of the over-peopled districts, then, of course, you are right; but I do not grant that, on the whole, pauperism has been on the increase; I am rather inclined to believe the contrary, although during the last two hundred years the population of Europe has almost doubled itself. Two things you should not lose sight of; in the first place, the increase in the means of transport having brought about a more equal distribution of food; and secondly, of nothing now-a-days being wasted, but, on the contrary, everything finding its way to where necessity exists. In consequence of a now universal free trade, every country produces exactly that which thrives best in its own soil and climate. Then, again, numberless acres of waste land have long been, and are still being, cultivated; whilst progressive science has rendered imperishable services to the practical agriculturist by pointing out to him various new modes and processes whereby to increase the crops and fruits of his fields. Thus, for example, we know now everything connected with the quality and quantity of all matters used in the cultivation of vegetables; moreover, every agriculturist has become, in our days, a manufacturer. To him the plants are the tools through means of which the so-called *inorganic* matter imbedded in the soil and atmosphere is to be worked and shaped into *organic* matter, *i.e.*, into matter fit for consumption; and therefore, as with any other manufacturer, his efforts are constantly directed towards obtaining the original *rude material* as cheap and as good as possible. Among this 'rude material' not a little is to be found that was formerly looked upon as mere waste, or, worse than that, mixed with the water or the soil of the towns, to the great injury of the public health. We are wiser now in the twenty-first century. Everything by which the produce of the fields can be increased is carefully collected, and life is thereby much better protected."

MODERN TELESCOPES.

I had already noticed, during the conversation, that our aërial conveyance had assumed a gentle swinging position; and when Bacon paused in his remarks, Miss Phantasia cried to me, "Do, now, apply your eye to these pseudo-cannons, and tell us, pray, where we are."

I found at once that those tubes which I had mistaken for cannons were enormous telescopes; but my mistake was pardonable enough, so far as their outward appearance went. They were certainly much wider, from which I concluded, *à priori*, that they must be powerful machines; but when I came to look through them, I discovered that their great width did in no way interfere with the sharp outlines of the images, and I was not only very much struck with their immense magnifying power, but at the same time with their great extent of the field of vision.

Following Miss Phantasia's finger direction, the first thing I saw before me through the telescope at the stern of the vessel was an immense city, which I fancied could be no other than Londinia, from whence we had started. A vast cluster or mass of houses presented itself, with the sharpest outline, in the somewhat dull background, but no idea of smoke; I therefore concluded that wherever coals were still used, one knew how to pass the smoke through the cowl or fire-grate in accordance with the wise Act of Parliament passed in 1850.

As I looked through the different telescopes which we had on board, I could not help admiring the scenery around and about us, which seemed to rush and rush on before our eyes whilst the ship was apparently lying still. Ascending, it was as if the earth went down beneath us. Shortly after, we caught the first glance of the sea, and right before us, opposite, we perceived the Belgian and French coasts. A black wire seemed to cross the narrowest strait of the Channel, so as to join the two opposite shores together.

CHANNEL BRIDGE.

As we came nearer I began to suspect that this wire might be a tubular bridge of some kind, and this surmise grew into certainty when Bacon assured me that a company had already been formed for the purpose of constructing a second one; "for," added my informant, "this one has become utterly inadequate to the extensive communication between England and the continent."

North Holland Submerged.

A slight north-north-easterly direction, and a few minutes sufficed to bring us near to my native home, which to us, from our vessel, looked like its outline in an atlas. Only how terrified I was to see that there was something wanting on the map. The whole province of North Holland,* *minus* a few diminutive islands,

---

* So little do we know of a country so worth knowing, that we daily commit ourselves by speaking of it as Holland. The kingdom of *the Netherlands*, as now constituted, is divided into ten counties or provinces, and two of these are respectively called North and South Holland. The former is the territory here alluded to; it includes neither Leiden, nor the Hague, nor Rotterdam. To speak of the Netherlands as Holland, corresponds to calling England Devonshire or Cheshire, and this particular terminology is the more amusing to the natives because

seemed to have disappeared. Not even trusting my eyes, I asked the " trunculant figure " who, Bacon said, was my countryman : Was the whole of North Holland imbedded in the sea ?

"So it is," was the answer. " That's the result of not heeding the advice of common-sense, prudent people. A handful of bragging citizens of Amsterdam insisted upon it, that they should have a canal right across into the sea. They had one already, in which they might have made some improvements, but that would not satisfy them. Well, after a good deal of agitation, they got their canal. How much it may have cost them I do not pretend to know ; no doubt a good deal more than many of them must have liked. However, now that they had it, it proved, after all, 'a fair-weather Jack ;' for as soon as the wind lost

with them it is a shibboleth of vulgarity. There never was a kingdom of *Holland*, except from 1806—1810, under Napoleonic rule, when the Dutch had lost their independence through that most dangerous scourge of nations, internal division.   T.

its temper—and such things *do* happen along our coast—the skippers did not venture to come too near to the shore. At the first November storm the harbour became full of sand, to clear which would have been to wash the negro.

"Thus the canal had had little power to benefit navigation. Still, matters did not come to the worst until, in 1980, the springtide fell in simultaneously with a storm such as the memory of living man could not trace. Sluices and dykes gave way, and North Holland, the greater portion of which was situated from one to five meters* below the mean level of the sea, was rapidly swallowed up by the raging element. Shortly after the play-going public of Rotterdam enjoyed a new drama, entitled 'The Horse of Troy.'"†

---

* The Dutch adopted the metric system for weights and measures simultaneously with the French; that is to say, at the close of the eighteenth century. Their meter is little more than three English feet.   T.

† In order to make this allusion to Rotterdam

"Terrible, terrible !" I could not refrain from exclaiming, although the man who supplied me with the "terrible" information did not appear to see it. I had already inferred from the latter part of his remarks that he was a native of Rotterdam, and this suggested to me the idea of once more looking through the telescope, and turning my looks towards the city where I had passed the earlier part of my youth. At first I did not feel at home at all. So much had the city of the Meuse enlarged itself into every direction, and so densely populated was the whole province of South Holland, that the towns of Leiden, the Hague,

intelligible to our English readers, we have to state a few facts. While Rotterdam has an excellent harbour, Amsterdam has not. From time to time the citizens of the latter city have devised all kinds of means whereby to remedy the natural disadvantage under which they labour. There is no lack of petty jealousies between the two great rival commercial cities of the Netherlands, and hence the allusion of dramatic rejoicings in Rotterdam at the misfortune of the competitor.   T.

Delft, Schiedam, and Rotterdam seemed to form but one large city.

Utrecht, too, appeared to have grown in extent. My eye fell accidentally on a bright dazzling spot, lighted up by the rays of Phœbus; and, anxious to find out what that was, I applied a stronger "oculaire" to the telescope, and soon recognised the golden sun of Justice, the well-known armorial bearings of the Utrecht University, on the top of a large and magnificent building. I thought that must be the University building, and inquired of the "trunculant figure;" but the latter answered curtly, "That's entirely out of my line, sir; those are things with which I have nothing to do." Fortunately for me, Bacon had heard my question, and he at once supplied me with the necessary information. "You have guessed rightly," said he; "when, after many years' waiting, there came at last a bill regulating the higher education in the Netherlands, some wealthy inhabitants of the city of Utrecht, at their own expense, founded this magnificent and imposing building, and by so doing furnished a living illustration of their interest in science, and of their affection for the *alma mater* to which many of them owed their education and social position."

Thanking Bacon for this valuable piece of information, I further ventured to inquire whether in the new educational bill the principle had been recognised "that it is a matter of perfect indifference where any candidate had obtained the knowledge required by the law, and that the state had no other right but to demand this of the candidate, that he satisfy the government examiners with regard to his abilities."

"Here you are doubtless touching a knotty point," answered my companion; "for this has been a matter of discussion for some time; and, strange to say, those that have given the most definite opinions on it are exactly those that were least competent to judge in the matter of public examinations. At first sight the principle you have laid down certainly appears reasonable enough. Those who, with you, appear to have accepted it, argue mathematically as follows : Given a certain quantity of linseed, then by the same press, and with the same amount of pressure, it will yield a certain amount of oil, and the latter will consequently indicate the exact relative value of the different kinds of linseed. It all amounts to this, to find a good press, one in regular working order. It is not otherwise with public examinations. These, too, are a kind of press, under which are to be brought the persons to be examined, and out of them are to be squeezed a dose of knowledge prescribed as the *sine quâ non* of their admission. It only requires to have a good examination press, and the results will always admit of comparison ; that is to say, they will be just and fair.

"But here a curious difficulty had to be surmounted. It is easy enough to construct presses from iron or wood that will work regularly ; but with examination presses that is altogether a different affair. Especially with regard to those for the higher branches of education the matter is not so easily procurable. And then there is another thing; neither are the examiners composed of wood and iron, nor are the students that have to be examined usually made of linseed; both classes of persons are more likely to be rational beings; the contract between them entails action and reaction, with thousandfold variations, so that there can never be any question of absolutely comparable results, least of all when the examiners and the examined are more or less strangers to each other. Leaving out other difficulties, there would still remain the very natural resistance which such heterogeneous elements would exercise towards each other, a resistance which will always be commensurate with the greater or lesser difference of interests in the parties concerned.

"In order now to overcome this difficulty, and to save the principle that "those aspiring to equal rights should satisfy equal conditions," the Government issued certain text-books in the form of examination guides. And what was the consequence? Industrious persons arose, and contrived to invent means by which to make those works essentially practical, and the examinations as light as possible; they composed little books containing questions and answers, something like catechisms, for every branch of science. This appeared to some people to be the height of examinatorial equality; but when, in spite of all this, the same complaints continued to be heard about the unfairness and arbitrary ways of examiners, the still more novel idea was mooted, whether it was not possible to solve the examination problem by a direct method, viz., physico-mechanically. For a long time past we had had speculums for the eye, for the ear, for the throat, etc.; why should we not succeed in inventing a speculum for the brain? There were already self-registering thermometers, barometers, magnetometers, photometers, etc.; why should we not have the self-registering enkephalometer? machines which in a few minutes, and by means of a few figures, would indicate the exact degree and amount of knowledge acquired by the individual to whose cerebrum the instrument might be applied! What a splendid invention, both for examiners and candidates, this would have been! Unfortunately the thing always proved impracticable; and the idea now ranks with the visions of perpetual motion and squaring of the circle.

UNIVERSITY EDUCATION.

" Meanwhile those exaggerated systems of examination had led to some experience, beneficial, though rather unpleasant. It gradually became to be noticed by competent persons that, in proportion as the students prepared for the required and enforced government examinations, there grew a dislike or decline of free study, an aversion to pure science, which is more dependent upon clear judgment than practised memory. And thus was lost the principal aim of all higher instruction which is not the 'training' for certain professions, but the complete and entire development of all the slumbering faculties of man.* The Dutch people began to see that they had been following the example of the Chinese, who surpass every nation under the sun in the length of their examinations; indeed, they found that they had run great risk of becoming the Chinese of Europe. It became generally recognised that every principle, however good in itself, may be 'overdone;' that examinations, however difficult to dispense with altogether, will always remain a sad necessity; and that it is perfectly chimerical to think of government examinations so arranged as to not only produce an universal and incontestable standard or measure of knowledge, but also to be a

* Although most of these speculations on university education would appear to apply to the author's own country, it cannot be denied by any one at all acquainted with the English seats of learning, that the whole is an unconscious but delightful bit of satire on the working and results of both Oxford and Cambridge.

T.

means of judging the theoretical and practical abilities of the candidates. It was further discovered that it was a gross error to suppose that government examinations were to be the stimulants for university study; in fact, that what was wanted was not means of discouragement, but of encouragement.˙ The human mind is like a liquid given to fermentation. Without leaven there cannot be any fermentation; and the latter is promoted by heat, depressed by cold. What you want in order to stimulate higher education in the higher sense of the word is a staff of competent tutors supplied with ample means for advancing and furthering knowledge in every possible direction; encouragement for all efforts to cultivate sound science, and nothing but the most beneficial results will accrue to society at large. Universities, at the dawn of their existence, were, as a rule, endowed with certain rights and privileges, like moral corporations; but these were swept away through the tide of progress having ceased to be adapted to the conditions of modern society. One right, let us say one duty, only remained vested in the universities, that of conferring degrees on its scholars after the passing of certain examinations; but the latter were subject, like all other examinations, to this, that they could never give a sufficiently satisfactory guarantee. Yet, while the defects of these were largely advertised, their advantages were often overlooked, until they were ultimately abolished, or replaced by the examining authority of government commissions. When at last it was found, after endless experiments, that people had been jumping from the frying-pan into the fire, one gradually began to recognise the truth of the French proverb, that '*Better* is the enemy of *good*,' and one came back to the old system slightly altered and improved. At the same time additional means were devised to render access to the universities, as seats of learning, more easy to deserving men; the fees were considerably lowered, and distinguished students received henceforth pecuniary assistance and support from those who were morally convinced that in the knowledge which they would acquire they would repay to society at large both capital and interest. And hence the number of scholars has so increased lately at your universities, that there no longer exists the semblance of necessity for admitting others to the exercise of the learned professions, than those who have enjoyed academical education. If to this some persons were to reply that such a restriction of the professional cyclus is rather hard upon those who have acquired their knowledge elsewhere, independent of the recognised universities, I would meet them with the counter-remark that the interests of the individual must give way to those of society at large, and that there is an intimate connection between the latter and the continuing prosperity of the universities."

I looked about me to see whether I could discover any more places of my native land. So far as I could see, the northern and north-eastern districts had almost doubled their population, for the towns looked twice their original size; but what struck me most was that the city of Arnhem looked apparently deserted. I was the more surprised at this, because I remembered quite well that about the middle of the nineteenth century the place had been rapidly increasing, both in extent and prosperity, owing to the many "old residents" who, having returned with colossal fortunes from India, purposed to pass the remainder of their days in this beautiful neighbourhood.

I must have allowed a suppressed cry of astonishment to escape me on noticing the crippled state of the city; for the "trunculant figure" once more addressed me in the native tongue: "Yes, sir," said he, "you are rightly surprised. From a large city Arnhem has become a third-rate town. Such things will happen when children attempt to govern their parents."

I did not exactly see the drift of this common-sense remark, until my countryman continued as follows: "I am going to tell you a story."

Loss of Dutch Colonies.

"Once upon a time a gentleman had a beautiful bird, and the beauty of this beautiful bird was this, that he laid every year a golden egg. Naturally enough, the man was very much afraid that this bird should escape, or perhaps be stolen from him. He therefore first cut its wings, and then put it into a solid cage. When the children of that gentleman grew up, they gradually became of opinion that the bird had not been properly treated by their father. One thought that some portion of the golden egg ought to be used in ornaments on the cage of the bird. Another hinted that not only should the cage be embellished, but also enlarged; the bird would then enjoy more liberty, and might perhaps lay two golden eggs in a twelve-month, 'in which case,' whispered he, 'I *myself* might come in for a little windfall.'

The third son went another step further; he would like to see the cage not only enlarged and gilded, but completely renewed as well; it ought to have much thinner bars to allow the bird more light and more air; this was its natural birth-right; for no bird was ever created to drag along its dreary existence in the dark. Finally, the fourth of the sons went so far as to say that it was 'a burning shame' to have cut the bird's wings. That was simply misusing the right of the stronger, and showed great want of foresight in him that had entrusted his 'governor' with the bird.

"The old gentleman was not a little embarrassed. He was not blind to the danger of all these juvenile counsels, but he was an indulgent parent, and never turned a deaf ear upon his children. First then the cage was gilded, then enlarged, and ultimately replaced by another, bran new, and as light as light could be. Meanwhile the bird's wings had been daily growing, and the animal at last managed to do that which every other bird would have done in its place. It escaped through the thin bars, and flew away."

"I fully understand; the bird's name was Java?"*

"Exactly so," replied the "trunculant figure."

"But what became ultimately of the bird?" I inquired.

"Ah, sir! it was after all a silly thing for the bird to fly away; it was not so badly off in its master's house; but birds will be birds. It had not flown far yet when it was attacked by two enormous birds of prey; they pulled it right and left with their sharp talons, and thereby injured one another severely. Of course the weaker bird lost a good deal of its plumage, and was bandied from the talons of one vulture into those of the other. At last the two monsters dropped their prey on the

---

* The principal colony of the Dutch in the East Indies, from which they derive no small benefits for their commerce and navigation. The island produces chiefly coffee, rice, sugar, and some tobacco.   T.

ground in piteous condition, whilst they pursued the combat between them with their own weapons, until both were so crippled and exhausted that there could have been no question on either side of looking after the weaker bird."

"If then I rightly understand your metaphor, France and England have both been compelled to let the island slip, and the Javanese are a free people by this time."

"Oh, free, of course; so is the dormouse," answered the Dutchman.

I suggested that his former remarks appeared to me to be more liberal.

"Those concerned the land, but not the people."

"Well?"

"The Javanese will never change their skin. Those of the present day are simply a few grades lazier than their progenitors. Since the last great war Java has been declared a neutral territory; all nationalities have equal rights to trade on it, and what do you think

7

has been the result? That of the few hundred-weights of coffee and sugar which the island continues to produce, scarcely anything finds its way to our own market; most of it goes to Marseilles and other parts of the Mediterranean."

At this point Bacon interrupted our conservative friend, and spoke as follows: "I am no trader, sir; but unless I am improperly informed, the Javanese people feel much happier now than when they were under the rule of the East Indian Company or the Culture System. It appears to me that possessions *which are not colonies proper* impose peculiar obligations on the temporary possessor, and that the latter is hardly justified in dealing with the inhabitants as the leech does with the patient. Wherever a superior race holds sway over an inferior one, it is the duty of the former to raise its inferiors to any such state of culture as they may prove themselves susceptible of. From the nature of things, such rule is always temporary, as history has often

taught us. The time must come when the
bonds will be rent asunder; but they will hold
so much longer together, and be so much more
easily dissolved, as the government has less
borne the character of oppression. A moral
ascendancy is on the whole the most powerful,
and that maintains itself best by fair and just
treatment of the weaker by the stronger. I
for one feel perfectly convinced that the only
reason why your country has even kept the
island as long as it has, was exclusively owing
to the few necessary reforms which your
government consented to make in the nineteenth century. But for those concessions,
Java would have been lost to you long before;
and with regard to the shifting of the market,
don't you think yourself, sir, that that was
chiefly brought about by the Suez Canal?"

"Perhaps so," replied the Hollander, not very
good-naturedly; "I won't argue the point with
you; you are an Englishman, and you fellows
think that you know everything better than
we do; this, however, I maintain, that if this

kind of thing is to continue, we shall go down as fast as we can."

I silently rejoiced to think that my telescopical observations had more than convinced me of this, that my countrymen had by no means so visibly yet come down, and I was inclined to conclude from this consoling fact that they had known in time how to apply the old Dutch proverb: "When the tide turns, turn your beacons." However, I did not venture to set my thoughts to words, for I should certainly have given offence to the "trunculant figure," whose solitary line of conduct apparently went along his own individual interests, and whose knowledge of political economy and of the rights of man was evidently at a very low ebb.

RAILWAY NETS.

During this somewhat prolonged conversation we had slightly deviated from our former course. We now moved along in south-easterly direction, and the native towns gradually disappeared from my sight. Looking towards

the east, I observed a small black speck which
obviously moved with great rapidity along the
surface of the earth, and seemed to advance
nearer and nearer to us. It became larger and
larger as it approached our conveyance, under
which it finally glided away. I had just had
sufficient time to recognise an immense train
of huge waggons in the fleeting meteor below
us. "From where," asked I, "did this train
start?" Bacon consulted his railway guide.
"That's the morning train," replied he, "which
left Pekin the day before yesterday, and runs
along the great central-east-west-line."

"From Pekin? Right across or over the
high mountains of Central Asia and Ural?"

"Oh, my friend, such obstacles have ceased
to exist in the twenty-first century. Surely
you yourself remember the piercing of Mount
Cenis? You will soon observe that what was
done in your time between France and Italy
has since been accomplished between Italy and
Switzerland."

There could be no doubt in the matter; for

the white-coated tops of the Alps already appeared at the horizon. The mountains themselves had not been affected by the hand of time or civilization, but the route went no longer across the Splügen, the Simplon, or the Saint Bernard, but underneath the mountain range, so that the same trains which we saw enter the tunnels on the Swiss side, made their appearance very shortly afterwards on the Italian side, and proceeded in their course through the plains of the valley of the Po.

I was in hopes that we should touch Rome on our way, for I was anxious to know what had become of that most venerable and ancient of cities; but I was sadly disappointed in my expectations.

GEOGRAPHICAL CHANGES IN EUROPE.

We floated over Venice, where the Italian standard waved from the top of St. Mark's, although I could recognise a few Austrian vessels by their immense double eagle. Now ascending, then again descending, it was often impossible for us to discover where we found ourselves, until I noticed Constantinople; but nowhere could I descry a single crescent, nor any other emblem that might have led me to conclude what Government had got possession of the ancient capital of the Eastern empire.

Crossing the Black Sea, and leaving the Caucasus behind us, we got a full view of the valley of the Euphrates; but I was again disappointed, in as far as I did not get anything to see in the shape of Eastern scenery. All the districts over which we travelled had quite a European cut about them. Nothing was there to show us that we were on another continent.

Among the buildings which I could clearly distinguish, one struck me as being in quite peculiar style. The numerous and large domes would have led me to suspect that it was a church or a mosque, but for the side wings and adjacent buildings, which looked like ordinary European houses, except that they were surrounded by colonnades. This edifice, or shall

I say this cluster of buildings, was situated on a rocky hill, whence the view was a most extensive one.

ASTRONOMICAL OBSERVATORIES.

I asked Bacon did he know what this edifice was intended for? He looked through the telescope, and replied, "Why, that is the famous observatory of Orumiah. I know it by an illustration of the building which I have in my library. I have not been there myself, but it must be well worth seeing."

"But how did they come to erect a building of such gigantic dimensions so far beyond the circle of civilization?"

"Simply for the sake of saving time," was the answer; "now-a-days only those spots are selected for astronomical observations where they can be made most conveniently and in the shortest possible time. In Europe the nights are scarcely ever sufficiently clear to use our now so powerful glasses to advantage. There, on the contrary, during several months of the year the sky is so bright and transparent that one can even with the naked eye observe the moons of Jupiter and the phases of Venus. This had been known many years ago to the American Stoddard, who even called Herschel's attention to the fact, but that was not the time for taking advantage of such excellent opportunities. Not until the beginning of this century was the foundation-stone to be laid of the *central observatory*, as it is called; the glorious building was erected at the joint expense of all civilised nationalities, the latter including the Persians themselves, who have long ceased to be behind us Europeans. I need scarcely assure you that this institution is amply provided with the most excellent instruments, and that it has a staff of scientific men second to none for making the necessary observations."

CALCULATORIA.

" Then at last," said I, " the science of astronomy has wandered back to the cradle of its infancy, the soil of Chaldea. But what has become of the once so celebrated observatories of Leiden, Greenwich, the Pulkowa, etc., etc. ?"

They have been changed into *calculatoria*, as in fact they had been already for some time past. Among them are distributed the observations made at the central observatory, and these they have to work out. At the same time these *calculatoria* continue to be of some use to the young astronomer; having there to encounter no end of difficulties, he may learn the value of the Latin adage, *Per ardua ad astera*, and so grow ultimately into a hard-working and accurate observer.

With regard to the practical results already obtained at the Orumiah observatory—in consequence of our knowledge of the celestial bodies having so considerably increased—I merely wish to call your attention for a moment to yonder map and the words printed underneath. I will rather not offend you by giving you any warning or advice in the matter.

TIN MINES IN THE MOON.

I followed the direction of his finger, and saw an immense "poster," on which I recognised at a glance the well-known lunar district of Tycho ; of course I was acquainted with its ring mountains and the bright silver beams radiating as from a common centre ; these were the words on the placard :

GREATEST DISCOVERY OF THE AGE !

INEXHAUSTIBLE TIN MINES IN THE MOON !

WHOSOEVER MEANS TO GET RICH

HAD BETTER ASSOCIATE HIMSELF WITH THE NEWLY

ESTABLISHED

MOON TIN EXPLORATION COMPANY, TYCHO.

I had already risen from my seat in order to examine the map, and to convince myself that the words were actually there. As I turned round, Bacon must have guessed or gauged the

degree of my astonishment; for he addressed
me as follows: "You apparently do not believe
in this kind of discoveries. Yet there is some
truth in the first part of the announcement;
nay, more perhaps than it is intended to con-
vey; for those tin mines are incontestably inexhaustible, and for this simple reason, that they
will never admit of being explored at all. Tin
mines, however, they are. Careful observations with the great parabolic reflector provided
with a hyperbolic 'oculaire' and a spectrum
analysis system for the reflected rays have
abundantly proved that those brilliant stripes
radiating from Tycho are nothing but metallic
tin. You will be less surprised to hear this
when you remember that the moon has neither
water nor atmosphere. So it is that metals
which on our earth generally present themselves in an oxydal condition of some kind or
other, on the contrary preserve their glossy
surface on the moon just as with us silver,
gold, and platina."

I now perfectly remembered that through

the invention of spectrum analysis in the latter half of the nineteenth century it had indeed become possible to discover metals and several other elements in the different celestial bodies, and I conceived some faint idea of the possibility of recognising, with the aid of greatly improved apparatus, even the chemical character of such small portions of the lunar surface as for example the Tycho stripes. The only thing quite inexplicable to me was this, how could there be people left in the twenty-first century so credulous as to believe in the exploration of tin mines in the moon by us, the inhabitants of the earth? When I put this question to Bacon, the following was his reply: "My dear sir, on this point, as on many others, men have not much altered. At all times there have been dupes, the victims of those that preyed upon them and of their own cupidity. The originators of this unlimited liability company know full well that there is no possibility of getting at the tin mines in the moon; all they want to explore is the cheque-books of

the public at large. In former centuries we
have had the same speculations; at that time
in the shape of tin, copper, and lead mines
that existed nowhere except on imaginary
maps, or in the form of landed estates, which
on closer examination of the facts often dwin-
dled down into pigstyes, or in the cultivation
of fertile soil, which turned out to be mere
wildernesses; very often a clever array and
combination of figures was resorted to, and
people were often brought to believe that one
and one are four, and that two times two are
ten. So it has been, and always will be. Think
of the very old maxim, *Mundus vult decipi.*
All that is required for such adventurers is an
elastic conscience, a good deal of "brass," and
a certain knack not to squeeze people's cre-
dulity too much, but to blind the masses by an
artificial coating of truth. In former times—
before science had to dispose of its enormous
resources—had any one proposed to fetch tin
from the moon, the commonest clown would
have looked upon him as an addle-pate; but

now-a-days so great is the number of recent discoveries and inventions, which to the un-educated mind savour almost of miracles, that many end in believing almost anything, and to my mind this is not to be wondered at. Start a company for parcel delivery by elec-tric telegraph, issue a prospectus stuffed with learned twaddle, and an elaborate quasi-scien-tific demonstration of your scheme—above all, hold out hopes of a wonderful profit—and you are sure to find shareholders enough."

UNIVERSAL SUFFRAGE, ETC.

"Poor children of man!" I thought. "Will you then always remain the same, always and for ever, always the slaves of your passions, and thereby the tools of those who take advantage of your weaknesses?" But my thoughts wandered into a different direction as soon as I noticed another placard simply containing this (although in monstrous figures and characters):

ANTI 1-2 LEAGUE.

Again I asked my companion for an explanation. "This is simply to call a meeting for
the purpose of forming a league to oppose the
one-two men." I was just as wise as before;
but Bacon continued his explanation with his
wonted courtesy. No mean introduction, however, was required to make the affair intelligible
to me. I first gathered then from him that
the right of universal suffrage had long since
been entrusted to men and women alike. At
first the privilege had been solely restricted to
such persons as were of age, but since then
the very consistent remark had been made
that this restrictive measure was very incon-
sistent indeed. Why had the money qualification been abolished? because it was osten-
sibly unfair that a man paying taxes to the
amount of two pounds should have a vote, and
another paying only £1 19s. 11d. should be
excluded from the poll. If the difference of
one penny constituted no vital distinction, why

not still further descend until we arrived at
zero? Now the clear-headed and far-seeing
people gradually learned to perceive that the
question of being or not being of age was
in itself a time-qualification, and these pio-
neers of progress began to argue as follows:
"Why, you grant the right of voting, of in-
fluencing for good or for evil the interests of
country and town, to doting old men, and you
withhold it from young persons in the vigour of
intellect, merely because the law has deemed
proper to call them "infants." You would
not scruple to enlist them as soldiers, and they
should have no vote in matters concerning
their own interests. Why should a man at
one and twenty be better than he was at
twenty? Was not Pitt England's prime mi-
nister on his coming of age? Is it not the
height of folly and absurdity to attempt to
determine by law at what period of life a man
will just have sense enough to be entrusted
with the performance of a duty which is the
birth-right of every free-born citizen? Such

laws are arbitrary and obsolete, a logical in-consistency, diametrically opposed to the grand and fundamental principle of equality before the law—aye, and a last remnant of those forms of paternal government which already in the nineteenth century began to be ridiculed and condemned; what could be opposed to such conclusive arguments? Some efforts were made, but those that attempted the struggle were cried down as unprincipled persons, weather-cocks, etc. A kind of compromise was arrived at; the period of coming of age was "recoiled," but still nothing yet would satisfy the zealots for the principle of logical consistency. Once more the date of majority was moved back, until even the babies were admitted by law to come into their "birth-right." The principle had been saved! the principle! and that was everything with the agitators. Difficulties there were involved in the principle no doubt, for some of the newly enfranchised babies could not walk, and others could not speak, and none could read or write.

Under these doleful circumstances the mothers claimed the right to go to the poll for those youthful interesting voters, and this exorbitant demand the league proposed to counteract. One was one, and not two. The most learned mathematicians went out of their way to prove that either was wrong, and neither was right, meaning that both were nonsense; but the mothers laughed heartily at such ironical demonstrations, "and," added Bacon, "the female party is by far stronger now than the male party."

WOMAN'S RIGHTS.

"Male and female parties!" exclaimed I, in utter astonishment.   "Have those then become the two contending parties in politics?"

"Naturally enough," replied he.   "Nothing else could have happened; it is the direct and natural consequence of the emancipation of women, whereby all rights have been granted them that were formerly exclusively accorded to men."

I could not help expressing my surprise at
such a result, and added that I was afraid that
it must have materially affected the relation
between the sexes.

A sarcastic smile seemed for once to ruffle
the placid features of Bacon as he laconically
answered, "Perhaps so." But Miss Phantasia,
who suddenly from a listener became a speaker,
made the following oral affidavit : "I will just
tell you the truth of the matter. I for one am
heartily tired of the present state of affairs,
and so are many of my sisters. When our
mothers and grandmothers first agitated and
ultimately carried these so-called woman's
rights, they certainly knew but half what they
were about. Equal rights suppose equal duties,
and equal obligations impose equal burdens.
Woman, demanding as a right that which men
had hitherto withheld from her, forfeited
thereby the privileges at one time acceded to
her by men. In the old works of fiction,
which to us are the sources whence we draw
the morals of bygone days, the man figures

conspicuously as the protector of woman ; any man laying any claim to the title of a gentleman treated a woman with respect and affability; hers was the place of honour in society ; she was both loved and respected, respected on account of her belonging to the weaker sex, loved as man's helpmate, not his competitor or rival. All this has changed now-a-days. We wished to protect ourselves, and we are less protected than ever. We have not taken our places by the side of the men, but against them, as they stand opposite us. Woman's weakness, once her strength, is no longer regarded by rival man, and now we begin to feel it. That which was formerly given us freely and willingly has now to be wrenched from our male opponents. The old feeling of chivalry has given way to the habit of rudeness. Politeness, though the word is not quite expunged from men's vocabulary, is seldom extended towards our sex. You must have noticed how, on going upstairs this morning, the men rudely pushed us aside so as to secure the best seats for themselves. This is a slight specimen of what happens and is tolerated in 'modern' society. Opposite man's violence is to be found woman's cunning, and the ultimate chances of success are pretty well balanced on both sides; but to whichsoever victory may fall, it can only be bought at the price of domestic peace and bliss, and of all those nobler qualities which then only will be properly developed when both sexes keep within the sphere allotted them by nature and disposition. Whatever we have gained in direct political influence we have lost in the indirect influence on the hearts of men, and it remains to be seen whether the gain has been greater than the loss. No, Stuart Mill, you who two hundred years ago were the first to put the dormant idea of female emancipation into the shape of words, and supported the agitation with all the weight of your name, you may have been a great philosopher, you may have known every possible thing about political economy, but you did not understand the human heart; and with regard to us women, you have played us a very bad trick."

That Miss Phantasia was earnest in her conviction was evinced by the unusual warmth with which she had spoken. Yet it appeared to me that she was a little too hard upon Mill. All that he and his followers undoubtedly intended to carry was that the right of voting should be extended to unmarried women, and to those that were possessed of some property. They could not be blamed for the extremes rushed into by their junior adherents. But there recurred to my mind the dreadful qualification scale, which had been lowered and lowered again, and I began to recognise that, here as elsewhere, all arguments have to give way before the so-called principles and logical consistency.

During our political conversation we had entirely lost sight of the Orumiah observatory, nor was I slow in observing that all the surrounding objects were gradually decreasing in size ; the barometer too, which depended from the ceiling of the saloon, had considerably gone down, whence I concluded that we were ascending rapidly, no doubt for the purpose of seeking a more propitious current in the higher atmospheric regions. Our ascent was unfortunately, but naturally, attended with disappointing circumstances; for all the places over which we travelled became more and more indistinct to our vision. It was not, however, until after some considerable time had elapsed that the surface of our planet became altogether of a greenish-blue colour. No doubt we were passing over the Indian sea. Of course the scene in the saloon was anything but lively under the circumstances. Most of the passengers ventured upon their slumbers, and I observed that with them, as with myself, respiration began to quicken, owing to the higher air in which we breathed. The snoring of the "trunculant figure" was utterly objectionable, not to say more. Even Miss Phantasia, lively and excitable as she was, had by this time fallen asleep, thereby depriving me of her animated dialogue with a pretty French lady with whom she had been discussing her pet subjects—poetry and the fine arts.   Bacon alone seemed absorbed in the reading of a learned dissertation "concerning the possibility of intercommunication between the various spheres of the universe by means of optic-telegraphic signals."   As for me, I recapitulated in undisturbed silence all the wonderful things which I had seen and heard of during the last two days, and I could not help saying to myself: if two single centuries can bring about such radical revolutions, what will the work of ages be?

THE NEW ZEALAND OF THE FUTURE.

At last I ventured to interrupt Bacon in the perusal of his learned work.   "Where do you think," I asked, "we are going to?"

To which he answered perfectly dryly: "I suppose we cannot be very far from New Zealand.   We have made a considerable *détour* through the upper air in order to take advantage of the atmospheric current which arises between the tropics, and then extends to the north and south and east successively, but now we are descending again. See how the barometer is going up."

Thinking on Bacon's words, I looked once more through one of the telescopes, and at some considerable distance I viewed two large islands barely separated by a very narrow strait.

"Now we are among our antipodes," continued Bacon. "New Zealand is the Great Britain of the Southern Pacific."

"But still she has not anything like a population so wealthy, powerful, and civilised."

"Still a better one than you would have imagined. Already New Zealand has several large cities with the same institutions for education and science and art as are to be found in Europe. She possesses an important commercial navy, has plenty of ore and coal mines, a splendid agriculture, innumerable herds of cattle, a flourishing industry, and an energetic population, chiefly of English descent."

" What has become of the Maoris ? "

"They have utterly disappeared, no one really knows where to. According to some New Zealand naturalists, they have died out; others imagine that they have migrated somewhere; others again are inclined to believe that a portion of the native inhabitants are of lineal Maoric descent. If this were the case, they must have considerably improved as a race; for the people here are now extremely peaceful. Should you ever visit Londinia in your travels again, you ought not to omit paying a visit to the National Museum ; there you will find two embalmed Maoris, a male and a female, the former beautifully tatooed. You will see them side by side with other embalmed specimens of the aboriginals, such as New Hollanders, American Redskins, etc., all of whom have long become extinct."

" Does the same apply to the inhabitants of all countries where Europeans have settled ? "

" No, only to those that are situated beyond the tropics; for the tropical regions, with the exception of the cooler mountain districts, are in the long run unsuited to the Caucasian race. The interior of Africa has still its original negro population; New Guinea is still inhabited by the Papoos, and many other islands of tropical clime are still occupied by the descendants of the ancient aboriginals, although they are rather on the decrease."

" Have those tribes that belong to the so-called inferior races improved at all in civilization ? "

" Not much. With all of them progress is slow, extremely slow. Some even hold the opinion that their progress is after all more imaginary than real; that is to say, that it merely consists of their aping some of the European manners and customs, and of these rarely the best. Still I believe I have sufficient ground to admit that they too are progressing, only that their progress differs essentially in its character from that of the Caucasian races."

Meanwhile we had reached so far the northern island of New Zealand that I was able to see through the telescope, not only the mountain tops but even the most densely populated districts.

Our fellow-passengers woke up one after the other, and Miss Phantasia asked me would I stay at the same hotel with them at Melbourne? "We go to the *Old-England*," continued she; "we have already ordered our dinner."

I answered of course that I could never too late part with such excellent company.

Bacon called the steward, and gave orders for us to be put down near Cape Maria van Diemen, from which a telegram should be sent to Melbourne.

Shortly afterwards we floated over New Zealand, and I was obliged to confess that Bacon had not said too much of that country.

Few districts in this world have been so largely favoured by nature. The large bays and gulfs were crowded with innumerable vessels apparently belonging to all nations. Of cities, towns, and villages, there was no end, and everything indicated the highest degree of prosperity.

Among the most conspicuous flags I noticed one very liberally represented; it had twelve suns on a blue field. Not knowing what they meant, I once more inquired of my guide: what country did they represent?

"That is the standard of the twelve united states of New Holland, which together form a federate republic," answered Bacon.

"A republic!" was my reply; "I always thought that New Holland belonged to the British crown."

"Such *was* the case," replied Bacon, "*at one time;* but the child has outgrown the mother. For ever so long the New Hollanders manage their own affairs. They are, as you are doubtless aware, of European descent. That is the

great difference between New Holland and the
East Indian islands, which at one time were
yours.   We have therefore parted on the very
best of terms, and the only bond that still
joins us together is that of reciprocal commercial interests.   The vast Southland has
become a powerful government; and if ever—
improbable as it is—civilization should migrate
from Old Europe, it still would know where to
find a centre.   You will soon become aware of
this on our landing."

We were rapidly moving.   New Zealand disappeared from our horizon, and in opposite
direction other districts seemed to emerge
from the sea.   That was New Holland, *the*
great Southland, the goal of our voyage.

Every passenger began to look after his
luggage.   The long extensive coastline lay
before us.   We were slowly and obliquely descending.   The objects on the surface of the
earth grew in size and distinctness.   It was
evident that we were approaching a large
city.   Melbourne it was.   A few moments

afterwards we heard a bustle and a kind of confused noise, only to be compared with the unfurling of sails and the untying of ropes. A violent shock followed, and—I woke up in my arm-chair.

THE END.

Watson and Hazell, Printers London and Aylesbury

INDEX.

9

www.ingramcontent.com/pod-product-compliance
Lightning Source LLC
Chambersburg PA
CBHW030604270326
41927CB00007B/1047